Take 5
Making Time For God In A Busy World

By
Darrell R. Ray

Columbia, South Carolina

Copyright 2020 by Darrell R. Ray

Take 5: Making Time for God in A Busy World by Darrell Ray

All rights reserved. This book is protected by the copyright laws of the United States of America. This book may not be copied or reprinted for personal gain or profit. The use of short quotations or occasional page copying for personal, or group study is permitted and encouraged. Permission will be granted upon request. Unless otherwise identified, Scripture quotations are from the King James Version. Copyright © 1982 Thomas Nelson Inc. Used by permission. All rights reserved.

THE MESSAGE, copyright © 1993, 2002, 2018 by Eugene H. Peterson. Used by permission of NavPress. All rights reserved. Represented by Tyndale House Publishers, a Division of Tyndale House Ministries.

The American Standard Version (ASV) of the Holy Bible was first published in 1901 by Thomas Nelson & Sons. Public domain.

Scripture quotations taken from the Amplified® Bible (AMP), Copyright © 2015 by The Lockman Foundation Used by permission. www.Lockman.org.

Scripture quotations taken from the Amplified® Bible (AMPC), Copyright © 1954, 1958, 1962, 1964, 1965, 1987 by The Lockman Foundation Used by permission. www.Lockman.org.

Scripture taken from the NEW AMERICAN STANDARD BIBLE®, Copyright © 1960,1962,1963,1968,1971,1972,1973,1975,1977,1995 by The Lockman Foundation. Used by permission.

Revised Standard Version (RSV), copyright © 1946, 1952, and 1971 the Division of Christian Education of the National Council of the Churches of Christ in the United States of America. Used by permission. All rights reserved.

[Scripture quotations are from] Common Bible: New Revised Standard Version Bible, copyright © 1989 National Council of the Churches of Christ in the United States of America. Used by permission. All rights reserved worldwide.

Scriptures marked NIV are taken from the NEW INTERNATIONAL VERSION (NIV): Scripture taken from THE HOLY BIBLE, NEW INTERNATIONAL VERSION ®. Copyright© 1973, 1978, 1984, 2011 by Biblica, Inc.™. Used by permission of Zondervan.

Scriptures marked TLB are taken from THE LIVING BIBLE (TLB): Scripture taken from THE LIVING BIBLE copyright© 1971. Used by permission of Tyndale House Publishers, Inc., Carol Stream, Illinois 60188. All rights reserved.

Scriptures marked NKJV are taken from the NEW KING JAMES VERSION (NKJV): Scripture taken from the NEW KING JAMES

VERSION®. Copyright© 1982 by Thomas Nelson, Inc. Used by permission. All rights reserved.

Scriptures marked NLT are taken from the HOLY BIBLE, NEW LIVING TRANSLATION (NLT): Scriptures taken from the HOLY BIBLE, NEW LIVING TRANSLATION, Copyright© 1996, 2004, 2007 by Tyndale House Foundation. Used by permission of Tyndale House Publishers, Inc., Carol Stream, Illinois 60188. All rights reserved. Used by permission.

Scriptures marked NSECB are taken from the NEW STRONG'S EXHAUSTIVE CONCORDANCE OF THE BIBLE: All Greek and Hebrew words are italicized. They are taken from The NEW STRONG'S EXHAUSTIVE CONCORDANCE OF THE BIBLE, James Strong.

Scripture quotations marked TPT are from The Passion Translation®. Copyright © 2017, 2018 by Passion & Fire Ministries, Inc. Used by permission. All rights reserved. ThePassionTranslation.com. 1990 copyright© by Thomas Nelson Publishers.

THAY - Thayer's Greek-English Lexicon of the New Testament. Complete and unabridged. Being C. G. Grimm (1861-1868; 1879) and C. L. W. Wilke (1851) Clavis Novi Testamenti Translated, Revised, and Enlarged, by Joseph Henry Thayer, D.D., Hon. Litt.D., Professor of New Testament, Divinity School of Harvard University, 1889. Electronic edition generated and owned by International Bible Translators (IBT), Inc., 1998-2000. Greek formatting modifications (such as adding diacritical accents) and improvements made by Michael S. Bushell, 2001.

Charles B. Williams, The New Testament: A Translation in the Language of the People. Boston: Bruce Humphries Inc., 1937. Slightly revised in 1950 (Chicago: Moody Press)

Dictionary.com, Book—Forest and Stream Sportsmen's Encyclopedia, Volume 62 pg. 276.Websters dictionary 1828.

Please note that this author and Change Publishers publishing style capitalizes certain pronouns that refer to the Father, Son, and Holy Spirit.

ISBN #978-1-7322629-2-8

Change Publishers Columbia, SC 29229

Machangepublishers@gmail.com

Printed in the United States of America First Printing, 2021

Cover photograph courtesy Shutter stock.

Additional Graphics courtesy Pixabay.com.

This Book Belongs To

Date

_____

Thank you for your support

Dedication

I dedicate this book to God the Father, Jesus the Son, and the Great Holy Ghost. I also dedicate this book to everyone who will read it. I decree and declare millions and millions will be blessed, and lives changed throughout the world and generations to come.

Maranatha
An Aramaic word that means "the Lord is coming" or "come, O Lord."

Apostle Darrell Ray

Acknowledgments

First, I would like to thank God the Father, Jesus His Son, and the Great Holy Ghost. Thank You for giving me the keys to spending time with You in prayer. As I practiced these principles You became more real to me and my life changed forever. My heart's desire to know You more intimately has been satisfied. Thank You for the divine connections and relationships You have placed in my path. Each has made an impact and a mark that cannot be erased.

I would like to thank you, my lovely wife, for all that you do for me, our family, and the Kingdom of God. Your steadfastness and unconditional love for us has made a difference in all our lives. Thank you for your labor of love for the Gospel and prayers for me as I walk out the call of God for my life.

I would like to thank my four daughters. You all are the reason I strive to be the Man of God for our family and generations to come. Each of you have impacted my life in a positive way. I am a blessed man because of you and love each one of you. Let God have His way in your lives and the lives of your family as He uses you to make a mark in the world that cannot be erased.

Thank you, Sparks Success Team, for being the best neighbors and friends anyone could ask for. This project would not have been completed without the two of you. You are a power couple for the Kingdom of God, and I am excited and happy for what God is getting ready to do in your lives. Eyes have not seen, nor ears have heard the great things God has in store for you.

I would like to thank my friend, Ty Green. Thank you for all your hard work and countless hours in helping us fulfill the vision and call of God upon our lives. Thank you for your artistic gift as you let the Lord blow and flow through your anointed work. Thank you for the Spirit of excellence that rest upon you as you do all that you do. It will never be forgotten. May God continue to use you and bless you in every endeavor as He gives you the desires of your heart.

Thank you, Melissa Penny and the late John Penny. You and your husband have impacted me, and my wife's lives forever. Your testimony and love for God continue to inspire us. Thank you for your help in editing and just your walk with the Lord, which gives us a modern-day example of living a life for Christ.

I would like to thank the rest of the Change Publishers' team. Thank you for your work of excellence and countless hours to bring this book to the body of Christ. I look forward to bringing hundreds of books to the body of Christ with our ever expanding and anointed publishing team.

Thank you, Barbie, for your testimony. You are an awesome friend and a mighty woman of God. May God continue to manifest your heart's desires as you continue impact on the lives you encounter.

Thank you, L.H., for your testimony. I am excited about what God has released in your life and manifesting for you. You truly have been a good friend throughout the years. I decree and declare your latter days will be greater than your past. Get ready for a culmination of the great things God has prepared for you.

I would like to thank Pastors Michael Moore and Angela Moore. Thank you for the time we served in ministry together. I gleaned great things from each of you. Pastor Mike, I have always remembered the words you spoke to us when we were talking about a publishing company. You said, "I want to see some books published, not just talked about." Well, here you go. Get ready for the floodgates of many more books coming from Change Publishers.

Introduction

This book will help you start developing your relationship with God. Many people say they do not have time. I get 24 hours in my day. How many hours do you get in yours? Let me help you with the answer to that question; You get 24 hours in a day. Let us explore a strategy to help you maximize your time so you can **Make a Change** and start incorporating and dedicating time for God.

Start off by spending five minutes with each step. Less than thirty minutes a day. If you get stuck on one step and God has you doing more, go with the flow. This is just a guide. This is not etched in stone. Be open to the Holy Spirit leading and guiding you as you spend time with God. Do not get convicted if you do not get through all the steps every day. The purpose is to spend time with God, not checking off a list. Do this for 21 days. I have heard it said, "it takes 21 days to create a new habit." Why not create a habit, or better yet, a lifestyle of seeking God? This is a format and an outline that has proven to be successful in my life and the lives of many others that I have shared this with. It is time to have success in your life. Will you take five?

Testimonials

I was in deep despair. I did not want to hope because it hurt to try to have hope. Anytime I tried to lift my head up and hope, it ended in additional pain. I had lost touch with Darrell after my college days. Then, out of the blue, he reached out and reconnected with me. He clearly saw the emotional and spiritual pit that I was in. He prayed for me, but I did not want to hear it. Undeterred, Darrell prayed to expel any demons that had a hold of my life.

After he finished praying, I immediately trembled, and I did not understand why. Darrell advised that the demons may have resided in me for a long time and the trembling I was experiencing was them now fleeing in fear before the power of God. Not too long after that experience, I heard a sermon on the power of hope. I decided to try to have hope again; specifically, a mustard seed's worth of hope. I had somehow held on to a mustard seed charm my father had given me when I was a child. I started wearing it again to remind myself that God can work with me if I at least try to have the smallest kernel of hope.

I then started doing Darrell's "Take 5" program daily. It very much helped me reconnect with God and my faith grew stronger during that time. I soon realized that having hope no longer hurt anymore. I started to look forward to the future. I started speaking positivity over my life and circumstances.

Eventually, I started being that positive voice of hope and faith to my friends who were in dark spiritual places of their own. The main take away for me from this experience is that I now seem to hear my spirit man a lot more clearly and regularly. I lean on God to help keep me strong and hopeful. Whenever thoughts of doubt and despair try to creep back in, my spirit man immediately chimes in with thoughts from the Word to rebuke any negative notions.

L.H.

Darrell Ray's understanding to help people grow closer to God is real and genuine. He is Spirit led and his teachings are simplistic, yet effective to guide people into a closer relationship with God.

You will find that one of the greatest things about this book is Darrell's down-to-earth voice, as he imparts his love for God's Word. He presents a knowledge and understanding to open communication with God through prayer, worship, the Word of God, thankfulness, and listening which has truly been life changing.

It is our habits of consistency; placing God first in our life, no matter how you are feeling. This book displays the simple teachings of bringing a closer relationship to our Father. It is impacting! Watch God move in ways you never thought possible.

Barbie

Contents

Dedication 7

Acknowledgments 9

Introduction 13

Testimonials 15

Chapter 1 Freshen Up 21

Chapter 2 Praise God 47

Chapter 3 Read the Word of God 59

Chapter 4 Prayer Part 1 69

Chapter 5 Prayer Part 2 89

Chapter 6 Listen 107

Chapter 7 Confessions 115

Chapter 8 Worship 131

Conclusion 136

Prayer of Salvation 138

Prayer for the Baptism of the Holy Spirit 140

Point of Contact 143

About The Author 145

Bible Translations 149

Chapter One

Freshen Up

We live in a world that is busy and full of distractions. The demands of day-to-day living can be overwhelming. Even though many of us attend church on Sundays, we find it hard to make time for God the rest of the week.

We may go to a midweek bible study, however, if truth were to be told, we rarely spend quality time with God. Life seems to keep us busy, distracted, tired, and constantly going from one thing to the next. Years after becoming a Christian, I found that the fire I had when I first became born again changed from a burning passion to a flickering flame. I did the things I was told to do as a Christian.

Take 5 Making Time for God in a Busy World

I read the bible, prayed, and went to church, but something was missing. After over 20 years of trying to reignite the zeal, I had a breakthrough one day while praying. The Lord spoke to me about the missing components and told me to write a book. So here it is.

Today is the beginning of the rest of your life. You have decided to make time for God in your busy life. You are about to come before God the Father, the creator of heaven and earth, whose son Jesus is King of Kings and Lord of Lords.

In the kingdom of God, you are considered one of the kings and lords. You are a joint heir with Jesus, so you must begin to live your life as He did. The bible shows us in the following verses your identity as a joint heir, kings, and priest:

And since we are his true children, we qualify to share all his treasures, for indeed, we are heirs of God himself. And since we are joined to Christ, we also inherit all that he is and all that he has.

We will experience being co-glorified with him provided that we accept his sufferings as our own.
—ROMANS 8:17 TPT

And hath made us kings and priests unto God and his Father to him be glory and dominion forever and ever. Amen.
—REVELATION 1:6 KJV

As a child of God, you must spend time with Him daily. Let us look at an example in the bible. Priest in the Old Testament had to purify themselves before going into the Holiest of Holies, the place where God's presence dwelled in the Tabernacle.

He shall put on the holy linen coat, and he shall have the linen breeches upon his flesh, and shall be girded with a linen girdle, and with the linen mitre shall he be attired: these are holy garments; therefore shall he wash his flesh in water, and so put them on.
—LEVITICUS 16:4

There has been a change in your life, so let us start fresh. Most people take a bath or shower every morning and night. You wash to get the dirt and grime of the day from your body so you can be fresh and clean. You are developing your quiet time with the Lord. Why not start your day fresh with your heavenly father early in the morning?

When you get up in the morning, brush your teeth and wash your face. Some of you are asking why? Morning breath is not the best when you wake up from a night of sleep. No need to pray with a filthy mouth.

Brush your teeth and get that unpleasant taste out of your mouth. Wash your face; some of you drool. Get the crust out of your eyes. Washing your face helps you to wake up. It feels refreshing in the morning. Now that you have done this in the natural, let's do this spiritually.

³Who shall ascend into the hill of the LORD? Or who shall stand in his holy place? ⁴He that hath clean hands, and a pure heart; who hath not lifted up his soul unto vanity, nor sworn deceitfully. ⁵He shall receive the blessing from the LORD, and righteousness from the God of his salvation.

—PSALM 24: 3-5

He that has clean hands are those whose hands are free from acts of sin. When you mess up, fess up. In other words, confess your sins.

If we confess our sins, he is faithful and just to forgive us our sins, and to cleanse us from all unrighteousness.

—1 JOHN 1:9

Notice he did not say "confess that you sinned," but confess your sins. Going to God saying, "Lord, I sinned, forgive me," does not have the same effect as saying what you did. For example, "Lord, forgive me for robbing you of my tithe and offering. I know your Word teaches me to return ten percent of my earnings to You and to give out of my 90 percent, but Lord, I used your money to go shopping."

When you hear yourself confess your sins, it brings it to the forefront of your mind and makes you conscious of doing the right thing. You have a new nature in you that is created after righteousness and true holiness; the real you, the inner man, the hidden man of the heart, that was born again.

There is nothing wrong with shopping, but make sure you are using money out of the 90 percent instead of the 10 percent that God requires you to return to him. Your hands may be free from acts of sin, however, when you see the word "and," it is a conjunction used to connect words of the same parts of speech, clauses, or sentences to be taken jointly.

So, in the above scripture, clean hands and a pure heart mean your hands must be free from acts of sin. Not only that, but you must also have a pure heart since the heart is the source of all evil. The following scripture in Matthew talks about this.

Freshen Up

For out of the heart proceed evil thoughts, murders, adulteries, fornications, thefts, false witness, blasphemies.
—MATTHEW 15:19

Unjust words and wicked acts are a result from the heart being impure. Get your heart right with God. Get rid of all hidden agendas, wrong motives, and unforgiveness. You are in control of this. God will not make you do this.

It is a decision you make to line your life up according to the Word of God, and not you trying to justify your issues with God. It is time for you to submit your life to God's will, which is obedience to His Word. The following scripture refers to God's desire for you:

I desire therefore that in every place men should pray, without anger or quarreling or resentment or doubt [in their minds], lifting up holy hands.
—1 TIMOTHY 2:8 AMPC

Before you come to God in prayer, freshen up. Empty yourself of anything that will not be pleasing to God. When you come to Him in prayer, He knows that you are not perfect, but what God wants is a willingness from you to allow Him to come in and help make you clean. He has washed us with His Word and Holy Spirit.

Let us look at proof of this in the Word of God. And it reads:

that he might sanctify her, having cleansed her by the washing of water with the word.

—EPHESIANS 5:26

The following verses from the book of Titus chapter three in the Message Bible translation make this point more clearly. It reads:

³But also, it wasn't so long ago that we ourselves were stupid and stubborn, dupes of sin, ordered every which way by our glands, going around with a chip on our shoulder, hated and hating back.

⁴But when God, our kind and loving Savior God, stepped in, ⁵he saved us from all that. It was

Freshen Up

all his doing; we had nothing to do with it. He gave us a good bath, and we came out of it, new people, washed inside and out by the Holy Spirit.

⁶Our Savior Jesus poured out the new life so generously. ⁷God's gift has restored our relationship with him and given us back our lives. And there's more life to come—an eternity of life! ⁸You can count on this.
—TITUS 3:3-8 MSG

Let God clean you from the inside-out. Work with the Holy Spirit as He recalls areas of your life that need to be submitted to the will of God. Just as a fisher cast a fishing line far away, cast away areas of darkness in your life as the Holy Spirit brings them to you.

Anger is an area of darkness that must be resolved. You may have had a disagreement or a fight with a fellow believer. You may feel justified in handling them in your anger, however, you notice they are still offended about the situation. You must resolve this. Matthew chapter five gives us an example of this below:

²¹ "You're familiar with the commandment that the older generation was taught, 'Do not murder or you will be judged.' ²² But I'm telling you, if you hold anger in your heart toward a fellow believer, you are subject to judgment.

And whoever demeans and insults a fellow believer is answerable to the congregation. And whoever calls down curses upon a fellow believer is in danger of being sent to a fiery hell.

²³ "So then, if you are presenting a gift before the altar in the temple and suddenly you remember a quarrel you have with a fellow believer,

²⁴ leave your gift there in front of the altar and go at once to apologize with the one who is offended. Then, after you have reconciled, come to the altar and present your gift.

—MATTHEW 5:21-24 TPT

God wants you to keep the air clear in dealing with your brothers and sisters in Christ. We are children of God, and we must walk in unity and

Freshen Up

---

love. It is time to let go of anger and be reconciled with one another.

Another area of relationship you need to keep clean is the area of your spouse. If you are married, there is a way to deal with one another as a couple.

¹Likewise you wives, be submissive to your husbands, so that some, though they do not obey the word, may be won without a word by the behavior of their wives, ²when they see your reverent and chaste behavior.

³Let not yours be the outward adoring with braiding of hair, decoration of gold, and wearing of fine clothing, ⁴but let it be the hidden person of the heart with the imperishable jewel of a gentle and quiet spirit, which in God's sight is very precious.

⁵So once the holy women who hoped in God used to adorn themselves and were submissive to their husbands, ⁶as Sarah obeyed Abraham, calling him lord. And you are now her children if you do right and let nothing terrify you.

⁷Likewise you husbands, live considerately with your wives, bestowing honor on the woman as the weaker sex, since you are joint heirs of the grace of life, in order that your prayers may not be hindered. ⁸Finally, all of you, have unity of spirit, sympathy, love of the brethren, a tender heart and a humble mind.

⁹ Do not return evil for evil or reviling for reviling; but on the contrary bless, for to this you have been called, that you may obtain a blessing. ¹⁰For "He that would love life and see good days, let him keep his tongue from evil and his lips from speaking guile;

¹¹let him turn away from evil and do right; let him seek peace and pursue it. ¹² For the eyes of the Lord are upon the righteous, and his ears are open to their prayer. But the face of the Lord is against those that do evil."

—1 PETER 3:1-12 RSV

Freshen Up

In the preceding verses we see the behavior of a Godly wife; she is submissive to her husband and because of how she behaves, she can even win an ungodly husband to Christ by how she walks and lives before God.

Many times when people see the word *submit* it has a negative connotation. Here the word submit means to be under subjection to your husband because you honor God's divine order of the family.

You honor his position as the head of the household and submit willingly because of that. Men, this does not mean that you treat your wife any kind of way. This would be detrimental to your prayer life. Notice verse 7:

"Likewise you husbands, live considerately with your wives, bestowing honor on the woman as the weaker sex, since you are joint heirs of the grace of life, in order that your prayers may not be hindered."
—1PETER 3:7 RSV

Men, you can have your prayers hindered by mishandling your wife. You must treat her as a fellow heir of the kingdom of God. Respect her and do not take her for granted. Your prayer life depends on this. Verses 8-12 instructs both husband and wife to watch how they speak to one another. God is not pleased when we speak harshly to one another as a married couple.

This does not mean that we must always agree with each other, but this means we do not have to disrespect one another by name calling and treating each other harshly.

God's ears are open to the prayers of the righteous, however his face is against those who do evil. Speak kindly to one another so that God's ears are open to hear your prayers.

Finally, unforgiveness is an area of darkness that many Christians have not dealt with. As I minister to people across the nation, I see the ugly head of unforgiveness rearing its head up everywhere. Many are locked in the prisons of the past hurts they have not gotten over; they halt their lives.

Unforgiveness changes into bitterness, deep hurt, anger, and the like. I am not taking lightly the things you have gone through. There may have been people in your lives that have done some horrendous things to you that even affect you today. Many of the hurts you are experiencing have come from those whom you have trusted and cared about. The Word of God is clear about forgiveness. It gives us simple instructions that we must obey.

<u>Mark 11:25</u> - *And when ye stand praying, forgive, if ye have ought against any: that your Father also which is in heaven may forgive you your trespasses.*

<u>Ephesians 4:32</u> - *And be ye kind one to another, tender-hearted, forgiving one another, even as God for Christ's sake hath forgiven you.*

Matthew 6:15 - *But if ye forgive not men their trespasses, neither will your Father forgive your trespasses.*

You must make up in your mind that you are going to obey the Word of God and forgive people. **Forgiveness is not an emotion, but a decision**. Decide today to obey God's Word and forgive people. It is ok to be real with God when you do this. The intensity of the pain caused by others is real, however, God's Word is true.

If you obey God's Word and forgive people, this will allow the love of God to enter your heart and take away the hurt which is the prison the enemy has left you in. Say this prayer to help you in this process.

Freshen Up

Father God,

I decide today to obey your Word and I forgive _____ (fill in the blank with the names of those you are forgiving). Please enter my heart and take away the hurt and pain. I love you God, more than I hate them. Fill me with your love and peace. Restore to me the joy of thy salvation. Help me daily to move forward and restore to me the time lost hurting over_____ _____(name the situation). I receive your Grace and move forward today, In Jesus' \Name, Amen.

As you get rid of these works of darkness, get clothed with God's armor. Do this with a sense of urgency. The faster you get this done, the more God will shine through you. I love the way the following two translations from Romans chapter 13 states this:

> [11]*Besides this you know what hour it is, how it is full time now for you to wake from sleep. For salvation is nearer to us now than when we first believed;* [12]*the night is far gone, the day is at hand.*
>
> [13]*Let us then cast off the works of darkness and put on the armor of light; let us conduct ourselves becomingly as in the day, not in reveling and drunkenness, not in debauchery and licentiousness, not in quarreling and jealousy.*
>
> [14]*But put on the Lord Jesus Christ, and make no provision for the flesh, to gratify its desires.*
>
> —ROMANS 13:11-14 RSV

> [11]*This is even more urgent, for you know how late it is; time is running out. Wake up, for our salv-*

ation is nearer now than when we first believed. *¹² The night is almost gone; the day of salvation will soon be here.*

¹³ So remove your dark deeds like dirty clothes, and put on the shining armor of right living. Because we belong to the day, we must live decent lives for all to see. Do not participate in the darkness of wild parties and drunkenness, or in sexual promiscuity and immoral living, or in quarreling and jealousy.

¹⁴ Instead, clothe yourself with the presence of the Lord Jesus Christ. And don't let yourself think about ways to indulge your evil desires.
—ROMANS 13:11-14 NLT

Notice that you put on the armor of light in one translation. We also know it as the shining armor of right living in the other translation. So, you are not getting clean to just get naked, but you are getting clean to arm yourself with the armor that God has provided for you.

Let us look at some more armor that you can put on as you prepare to do battle against your enemies, as well as get ready for prayer. The following verses are from Ephesians Chapter six:

[10]Finally, my brethren, be strong in the Lord, and in the power of his might. [11]Put on the whole armor of God, that ye may be able to stand against the wiles of the devil.

[12]For we wrestle not against flesh and blood, but against principalities, against powers, against the rulers of the darkness of this world, against spiritual wickedness in high places.

[13]Wherefore take unto you the whole armor of that ye may be able to withstand in the evil day, and having done all, to stand. [14]Stand therefore, having your loins girt about with truth, and having on the breastplate of righteousness;

[15]And your feet shod with the preparation of the gospel of peace; [16]Above all, taking the shield of faith, wherewith ye shall be able to quench all the fiery darts of the wicked. [17]And take the helmet

of salvation, and the sword of the Spirit, which is the word of God.
—EPHESIANS 6: 10-17

Verse 10 in Ephesians 6 talks about putting on the whole armor of God. This armor consist of truth covering your loins, righteousness as your breastplate, your feet shod with the Gospel of Peace, salvation as your helmet, faith as your shield and The Word of God as your sword. Notice this armor has no backplate. God never intended for you to turn and run from the enemy. Also notice that you have a sword.

Many times, you think of a sword as an offensive weapon however, you can use a sword as a defensive weapon to block attacks sent against you. Jesus did this when he was being tested in the wilderness by Satan. Every time Satan attacked him with temptation, Jesus replied, with His sword, the Word of God, "It is written." He used the Word of God to neutralize every attack of Satan in the following passage from the fourth chapter of Matthew, beginning with verse three:

³And when the tempter came to him, he said, If thou be the Son of God, command that these stones be made bread. ⁴But he answered and said, It is written Man shall not live by bread alone, but by every word that proceedeth out of the mouth of God.

⁵Then the devil taketh him up into the holy city, and setteth him on a pinnacle of the temple, ⁶and saith unto him, If thou be the Son of God, cast thyself down: for it is written, He shall give his angels charge concerning thee: and in their hands they shall bear thee up, lest at any time thou dash thy foot against a stone.

⁷Jesus said unto him, It is written again, Thou shalt not tempt the Lord thy God. ⁸again, the devil taketh him up into an exceeding high mountain, and sheweth him all the kingdoms of the world, and the glory of them;

⁹and saith unto him, All these things will I give thee, if thou wilt fall down and worship me. ¹⁰Then saith Jesus unto him, get thee hence, Satan

Freshen Up

for it is written, thou shalt worship the Lord thy God, and him only shalt thou serve. ⁱⁱThen the devil leaveth him, and behold, angels came and ministered unto him.
—MATTHEW 4:3-11

Here is another set of armor you can put on.

⁷Night is the time when people sleep, and drinkers get drunk. ⁸But let us who live in the light be clearheaded, protected by the armor of faith and love, and wearing as our helmet the confidence of our salvation. ⁹For God chose to save us through our Lord Jesus Christ, not to pour out his anger on us.
—1 THESSALONIANS 5:7-9

Faith and love are the armor, combined with the helmet of salvation again. Notice how the helmet of salvation continues to guard the head. The head is an area that contains your brain and if wounded or struck could affect the rest of the body negatively. Without a head, the entire body would not function properly. Notice the helmet is salvation. The word salvation in Ephesians comes from the Greek word "***Sōtērios***", which means:

−*saving, bringing salvation.*

−*he who embodies this salvation, or through whom God is about to achieve it.*

−*the hope of (future) salvation.*
(Strong's Hebrew and Greek dictionary)

I love the middle definition, "he who embodies this salvation, or through whom God is about to achieve it." When I think of that definition of salvation, I see God working through the one who uses salvation as a helmet.

In 1 Thessalonians 5:7, the word "salvation" means:

Sōtēria

−*rescue or safety.*

−*deliver, health, salvation, save, saving.*
(Strong's Hebrew and Greek dictionary)

Freshen Up

This definition of the Word salvation goes deeper in the preceding verse. It changes to the feminine of a derivative of *Sōtērios.*

This helmet of salvation is bringing about deliverance, health, rescue, and safety. Keeping you in your right mind as you are in the battle against the adversary that comes to war with you in your mind. When the enemy attacks you, he attacks you first in your mind.

He wants you to doubt the Word of God, so he sows seeds, which are words of doubt, into your head to cause you to be defeated in your thought process. As you are wearing your helmet of salvation, cast down every thought and imagination that comes against the Word of God that has been planted in your heart and mind. Now you are clean and dressed for service.

Always remember, preparation time is not lost time. Sometimes you must slow down to speed up. Before rushing into the presence of God any kind of way, take time to come before him the right way by laying aside every weight and sin that so easily besets you. Cleaning yourself by emptying yourself of things that do not please God is a sign of humility and lets God see the sincerity of your heart. Putting on the Armor of light (right living) and the whole armor of God, will help you against the things the enemy throws at you to keep you bound.

Chapter Two

Praise God

O magnify the LORD with me and let us exalt his name together.
—PSALM 34:3 KJV

It is time to praise God! The word magnify means to make (something) greater or appear larger. As you magnify the Lord, He gets bigger and your issues get smaller. Our God is bigger than everything that is going on in your life. He is bigger than all your problems, issues, and circumstances.

In the Old Testament, when God wanted to reveal Himself to man, He revealed Himself through one of His redemptive names. One of the Hebrew names for God is "Jehovah." A word or phrase which described God's attributes to the children of Israel followed the Word "Jehovah." When the children of Israel needed a Healer, God revealed Himself as Jehovah-Rapha (The Lord Who heals). Whatever they needed; God revealed Himself as that.

> *And said, If thou wilt diligently hearken to the voice of the LORD thy God, and wilt do that which is right in his sight, and wilt give ear to his commandments, and keep all his statutes, I will put none of these diseases upon thee, which I have brought upon the Egyptians: for I am the LORD that healeth thee.*
> —EXODUS 15:26

In Exodus 17:15, Moses recognized the Lord was Israel's banner under which they defeated the Amalekites. Moses built an altar and named it Jehovah-Nissi (The Lord our Banner).

> *And Moses built an altar and called the name of it Jehovah-nissi.*
> —EXODUS 17:15

Praise God

In battle, opposing nations would fly their own flag on a pole at each of their front lines. This gave soldiers a focal point and hope. This is what God was to Israel, their banner reminding them He was with them on the front line.

There are several ways man reveals himself to God. One way is through Praise. There are nine original words used to describe praise in the Old Testament Hebrew language. This is awesome. The number (9) symbolizes divine completeness or conveys the meaning of finality. Let's look at these words, their definitions, and examples of them used in scripture:

Yâdâh, yaw-daw'; Hold out the hand; physically, especially to revere or worship (with extended hands). Expresses gratitude, thankfulness, and surrender.

Judah, thou art he whom thy brethren shall praise: thy hand shall be in the neck of thine enemies; thy father's children shall bow down before thee.
—GENESIS 49:8

Hâlal, haw-lal'; To shine; hence to make a show, to boast; to celebrate extravagantly. Root of the word "hallelujah" which means "praise (halla) to jah (God)". Expresses joy, jubilation, and celebration.

<u>Praise</u> ye the LORD. Praise God in his sanctuary: <u>praise</u> him in the firmament of his power.
—PSALM 150:1

Let everything that hath breath <u>praise</u> the LORD. <u>Praise</u> ye the LORD.
—PSALM 150:6

Tehillâh, teh-hil-law'; Song or hymn of praise; Singing scripture to instruct and encourage.

Who is like unto thee, O LORD, among the gods? Who is like thee, glorious in holiness, fearful in <u>praises</u>, doing wonders?
—EXODUS 15:11

For in the days of David and Asaph of old there were chief of the singers, and songs of <u>praise</u> and thanksgiving unto God. *—NEHEMIAH 12:46*

Praise God

Bârak, baw-rak' to kneel; by implication to bless God (as an act of adoration); Kneel, bless the Lord. Expresses humility.

And <u>blessed</u> be the most high God, which hath delivered thine enemies into thy hand. And he gave him tithes of all.
—GENESIS 14:20

And I bowed down my head, and worshipped the LORD, and <u>blessed</u> the LORD God of my master Abraham, which had led me in the right way to take my master's brother's daughter unto his son.
—GENESIS 24:48

Zâmar, zaw-mar'; to touch the strings or parts of a musical instrument, i.e., play upon it; to make music, accompanied by the voice. Make music by striking the fingers on strings or parts of a musical instrument.

When we play instrumentally to facilitate a holy atmosphere, it's not just church music, it's zamar.

My heart is fixed, O God, my heart is fixed: I will sing and give <u>praise</u>.
—PSALM 57:7

A Song or Psalm of David. O God, my heart is fixed; I will sing and give <u>praise</u>, even with my glory.
—PSALM 108:1

<u>Tôwdâh</u>, to-daw'; properly, an extension of the hand, i.e., specifically, a choir of worshippers: confession, (sacrifice of) praise, thanks (-giving, offering). The raised hand. Expresses adoration.

Judah, thou art he whom thy brethren shall <u>praise</u>: thy hand shall be in the neck of thine enemies; thy father's children shall bow down before thee.
—GENESIS 49:8

I will <u>praise</u> the LORD according to his righteousness: and will sing praise to the name of the LORD most high.
—PSALM 7:17

Praise God

Shâbach, shaw-bakh'; Shout praise. Expresses confidence in God's ability. To address in a loud tone, i.e. (specifically) loud.

Because thy loving-kindness is better than life, my lips shall <u>praise</u> thee.
—PSALM 63:3

One generation shall <u>praise</u> thy works to another and shall declare thy mighty acts.
—PSALM 145:4

Tâqa, taw-kah' Clap, applaud. Expresses joy and victory.

To the chief Musician, A Psalm for the sons of Korah. O <u>clap</u> your hands, all ye people; shout unto God with the voice of triumph.
—PSALM 47:1

There is no healing of thy bruise; thy wound is grievous: all that hear the bruit of thee shall <u>clap</u> the hands over thee: for upon whom hath not thy wickedness passed continually?
—NAHUM 3:19

Kârar, kaw-rar'; a primitive root; to dance (i.e., whirl): — dance (-ing).

And David <u>danced</u> before the LORD with all his might; and David was girded with a linen ephod.
—2 SAMUEL 6:14

And as the ark of the LORD came into the city of David, Michal Saul's daughter looked through a window, and saw king David leaping and <u>dancing</u> before the LORD; and she despised him in her heart.
—2 SAMUEL 6:16

A simple definition of Praise is thanking God for what He has done. Make it personal. Reflect on what God has done in your life. We have a cliché in the church, "When I think of the goodness of Jesus and ALL that He's done for me, my soul cries out Hallelujah, I thank God for saving me".

Start off with the simple things: Lord, I thank You because I have clothes to put on. Thank You for waking me up another day. Thank You for

Praise God

having breath in my body. Thank You for the bed I slept in last night. I thank You for what you did on the cross for me, dying so I might live. I thank you for your precious blood that You shed for me and by Your stripes I am healed.

As you start off with the simple things to praise God for, you stir up the Holy Spirit who is on the inside of you. He brings up other things that God has done in your life and you get excited! You are excited because you know if He did it before, He can and will do it again.

Praise is a powerful weapon in your arsenal. It ushers in the presence of Almighty God. Your praise builds a throne for God and He sits in the midst.

His essence and glory cause the atmosphere to shift. Your circumstances and situations will bow down at the entrance of His Glory. In this place, fear turns to faith. Hopelessness turns to joy unspeakable and full of Glory.

For the weapons of our war fare are not carnal, but mighty through God to the pulling down of strong holds;
—2 CORINTHIANS 10:4

For the weapons of our warfare are not worldly but have divine power to destroy strongholds;
—2 CORINTHIANS 10:4 RSV

But thou art holy, O thou that inhabitest the praises of Israel.
—PSALM 22:3

Praise shifts the surrounding atmosphere to a heavenly dominion that evil cannot stand. When you praise there should be a fire in your heart and a focus in your mind. You should think about what God has done and is getting ready to do.

When you pray, believe that you already received what you are praying for and then you will have it. That is why you can praise God in advance.

Praise God

For thou art not a God that hath pleasure in wickedness: neither shall evil dwell with thee.
—PSALM 5:4

And when they began to sing and to praise, the LORD set ambushments against the children of Ammon, Moab, and mount Seir, which were come against Judah; and they were smitten.
—2 CHRONICLES 20:22

And when he had consulted with the people, he appointed singers unto the LORD, and that should praise the beauty of holiness, as they went out before the army, and to say, Praise the LORD; for his mercy endureth forever.
—2 CHRONICLES 20:21

We have a faithful God who keeps his promises. It is ok to give God praise in advance because He is Faithful.

> *If we are faithless [do not believe and are untrue to Him], He remains true (faithful to His Word and His righteous character), for He cannot deny Himself.*
> —2 TIMOTHY 2:13 AMP

Your praise should be deliberate and focused. If you really want to raze (to tear down; demolish; level to the ground: to scrape, cut, or shave off: Erase) hell in warfare, combine multiple ways of praising God. There are at least 729 combinations for you to praise God.

You can kneel, clap your hands, and shout Hallelujah all at the same time. God is on your side. Energize your mornings with a fiery shout of praise to our God most high!

Chapter Three

Read the Word of God

When you are born again, your Spirit man is made new. It is not fixed, it is not renovated, but made new. You are made in the image and likeness of God. God is three in one: God the Father, God the Son, and God the Holy Spirit. Man is three in one: spirit, soul, and body. The real you, (the inner man) is Spirit. You have a soul which houses the faculty of your mind and your emotions. You live in a body. Your body is your earth suit that allows you to function in the physical world around you. The bible says God is a Spirit:

> *God is a Spirit: and they that worship him must worship him in spirit and in truth.* —JOHN 4:24

Because you are made in the image and likeness of God, you are a Spirit [the real you]. Just as your natural body needs food to thrive, so does your spirit man. Many Christians are malnourished and suffer malnutrition in the spirit because of what they are feeding their spirit man. Jesus said, "man should not live by bread alone but by every Word that proceeds out the mouth of God."

But he answered and said, it is written, Man shall not live by bread alone, but by every word that proceedeth out of the mouth of God.

—MATTHEW 4:4

Many people are existing but not living. They are filling themselves up with junk food. Junk food is the things of this world which satisfies your lust and keeps you from the things of God. You can eat the Word of God or the word of the World system. The Word of God brings life to your Spirit. The things of the world system bring clutter and keeps you focused on yourself.

Read the Word of God

The world system is just that; a system to manipulate and control your soul. Your soul is your mind, will, intellect, and emotions. One tool used to program you is television. If you slow down and say the word **television** slowly, it has a hidden message, **"Tell-A-Vision"**. Through television, an ungodly and unruly mindset is being pumped out to you to change your morality.

Television programming feeds your mind images designed to change your thinking and force you to accept another way of thinking.

Your mind is like a computer; if you put junk in, you will get junk out. Television uses repetition to deprogram your morality by flooding it with repeated information of ungodly ways of living and thinking. By contrast Romans 12 teaches:

And be not conformed to this world: but be ye transformed by the renewing of your mind, that ye may prove what is that good, and acceptable, and perfect, will of God.
—ROMANS 12:2

You must keep your mind renewed with the Word of God daily, so you can keep the weeds of the world system from choking out the Word of God which brings life. The Just shall live by faith.

For therein is the righteousness of God revealed from faith to faith: as it is written, <u>the just shall live by faith</u>.
— ROMANS 1:17

But that no man is justified by the law in the sight of God, it is evident: for, <u>the just shall live by faith</u>.
— GALATIANS 3:11

Now <u>the just shall live by faith</u>: but if any man draw back, my soul shall have no pleasure in him.
— HEBREWS 10:38

The statement "The just shall live by faith", is stated three times in the Word of God. It must be important. What is faith?

Now faith is the assurance (the confirmation, the title deed) of the things [we] hope for, being the

Read the Word of God

proof of things [we] do not see and the conviction of their reality [faith perceiving as real fact what is not revealed to the senses].
—HEBREWS 11:1 AMP

In plain English, faith is the evidence, the documentation of the things we cannot see in this physical world around us. How do you get faith?

So then faith cometh by hearing, and hearing by the word of God.
—ROMANS 10:17

When you are hearing the Word of God, you are receiving faith. In some places in the bible faith and the Word of God are the same; you cannot detach one from the other. Faith is the Word of God. The Word of God is Faith. If the two are the same in some places in the bible, I could use both interchangeably and the meaning would be the same. Let us dig deeper into this statement.

Now <u>faith</u> is the substance of things hoped for, the evidence of things not seen.
—HEBREWS 11:1

Now the <u>Word of God</u> is the substance of things hoped for, the evidence of things not seen.

The Word of God represents the title deed. It is the physical evidence of the thing you are believing God for. If you have the Word of God as your title deed, you have proof of the thing God promised you. When a person dies, many of them leave a Last Will and Testament.

The word *testament* defined: Testament is proof or evidence that something exists or is true Law:

the legal instructions in which you say who should receive your property, possessions, etc., after you die.

A Last Will and Testament allows you to communicate your wishes and make things easier for the people you care about. Creating a Last Will and Testament as part of your estate plan will ensure all you leave behind, including the care of your children, will be taken care of according to

Read the Word of God

your wishes. God gave us His Word. He gave us an old testament and a new testament. He sent his Son Jesus, who died to activate His will in the earth.

Whereby are given unto us exceeding great and precious promises: that by these ye might be partakers of the divine nature, having escaped the corruption that is in the world through lust.
—2 PETER 1:4

For you to partake in the divine nature of God, you must have the divine nature of God's food, which is the Word of God. The Word of God will feed your spirit man the nutrients needed to live the God kind of life.

It is the spirit that quickeneth; the flesh profiteth nothing: the words that I speak unto you, they are spirit, and they are life.
—JOHN 6:63

The inner man [the real you] is a spirit being. Your spirit being needs the life of the Word of God to live the way God designed us to live Like Him!

Faith comes by hearing and hearing by the Word of God. Revelation comes by reading the Word of God and illumination from the Holy Spirit. I like to be productive, so I read the Word of God out loud to increase my faith and receive revelation at the same time.

Reading and meditating on the Word of God daily has benefits. Many people want to be successful.

This book of the law shall not depart out of your mouth, but you shall meditate on it day and night, that you may be careful to do according to all that is written in it; for then you shall make your way prosperous, and then you shall have good success.
—JOSHUA 1:8 RSV

Read the Word of God

As you **read** the Word of God, **receive** the Word of God, **act** on the Word of God, and **do** the Word of God, your life will transform day after day. You will be a child of God whose life reflects God. You will love like Him, talk like Him, and live like Him.

> *¹So, here's what I want you to do, as God helps you: Take your everyday, ordinary life—your sleeping, eating, going to work, and walking around life—and place it before God as an offering. Embracing what God does for you is the best thing you can do for him.*
>
> *²Don't become so well-adjusted to your culture that you fit into it without even thinking. Instead, fix your attention on God. You'll be changed from the inside out. Readily recognize what he wants from you, and quickly respond to it. Unlike the culture around you, always dragging you down to its level of immaturity, God brings the best out of you, develops well-formed maturity in you.*
>
> —ROMANS 12:1-2 MSG

Chapter Four

Prayer Part 1

After you have read the Word of God, you are now in a suitable position to pray, because you have armed yourself with the knowledge of God's Word. Before you can pray, you need to understand what is prayer?

Prayer in simple terms is communicating with God. First, to have a successful prayer life, you need to know what God has said in His Word, which is His will. When the will of God is known, faith can begin. Knowing what God has said in His Word concerning a situation gives you the confidence to believe He will do it for you.

Second, you need to understand that there are different types of prayers. Unfortunately, many people have prayed and not received answers because they have not known this. There are various types of prayers in the bible, just like there are distinct types of board games. The various kinds of prayer have their own set of rules, as do the distinct board games. You cannot play chess using checker rules.

You cannot play Monopoly using Backgammon rules. Doing so would cause much confusion, thus accomplishing nothing. This is what many people are doing when they pray. They are praying prayers using the wrong set of rules for the type of prayer they are praying. (picture prayer being like a set of keys).

You use original keys on your key chain to unlock different locks. You cannot use the same key you used to unlock your house, to start your car; Two original keys with two separate purposes. Prayer is the same way. You use different prayers for distinct purposes, as stated in the verse below.

First of all, then, I urge that petitions (specific requests), prayers, intercessions (prayers for others) and thanksgivings be offered on behalf of all people, for kings and all who are in [positions of] high authority, so that we may live a peaceful and quiet life in all godliness and dignity.

—1 TIMOTHY 2-3 AMP

We can use several kinds of prayers together when praying, but we must know what we are doing. It is important to define the distinct prayers so we can apply them properly, even if we combine them occasionally.

Prayer of Faith/Petition:

Webster's dictionary defines the word "petition":

1. An earnest request: entreaty

2. a. a formal written request made to an official person or organized body (as a court)

b. a document embodying such a formal written request

3. Something asked or requested

The prayer of faith/petition is a prayer between you and God. It is you asking God for a result.

Therefore, I tell you, whatever you ask in prayer, believe that you have received it, and it will be yours.
—MARK 11:24 RSV

The key to understanding this prayer is simple; you believe that you have it (the thing you are praying for) before you get it. You believe you have it when you pray. You must receive it and believe it is done after you pray; not when you see it and not when you feel something, but when you pray. The instant you pray, it is yours. God answers immediately.

For example, let's look at the book of Daniel:

Then said he unto me, Fear not, Daniel: for from the first day that thou didst set thine heart to un-

Prayer Part One

derstand, and to chasten thyself before thy God, thy words were heard, and I am come for thy words. But the prince of the kingdom of Persia withstood me one and twenty days: but, lo, Michael, one of the chief princes, came to help me; and I remained there with the kings of Persia.

—DANIEL 10:12-13

Daniel's prayer was heard and answered the moment he prayed. There was a blockage in the heavens from the prince of the kingdom of Persia, a demonic spirit. The Arch Angel Michael had to fight through the heavenly realm to help the angel get the answer to Daniel.

When you pray, God answers immediately in the spirit realm. Sometimes it takes a while to manifest in our physical realm because of the demonic hinderances in the spiritual realm. You must not lose faith!

Believe and you shall receive; doubt and you will do without. You must press into prayer until your answer comes.

Prayer of Agreement:

Again, I say to you, if two of you agree on earth about anything they ask, it will be done for them by my Father in heaven.
                            —MATTHEW 18:19 RSV

The emphasis on this kind of prayer is agreement. Agreement is the being of one mind with others. For this prayer to work, everyone involved MUST agree. It needs to be clear of what you are coming into agreement about. If you come to me asking me to agree on an unspoken prayer request, this is not in agreement. How can I agree with you if I do not know what you are asking? There is no such thing as an unspoken prayer. If it is not spoken, it is nothing but a thought. Jesus said to the disciples:

And he said unto them, When ye pray, <u>SAY</u>, Our Father which art in heaven, Hallowed be thy name. Thy kingdom come. Thy will be done, as in heaven, so in earth.   —LUKE 11:2

Prayer Part One

You must give voice to prayer. For clarity, I ask, "what do you want me to pray for?" Once I have clarity, I can now come into an agreement with you in prayer. This prayer is good for married couples to transform their households. Who better to come into agreement with, than the person you have committed your life to?

Prayer of Consecration and Dedication:

And he withdrew from them about a stone's throw, and knelt down and prayed, "Father, if thou art willing, remove this cup from me; nevertheless not my will, but thine, be done"
—LUKE 22:41-42 RSV

Jesus was getting ready to face His crucifixion and death. The thought of going through this brought a lot of anxiety and stress. Jesus was asking, "God, if there is any other way for this to happen, can we do it that way?" But the point for us is, **"nevertheless, not my will, but thine, be done."**

Sometimes in your life, when you seek direction from God because you want His path, you may not be clear on what you can or should do. You have **good** choices to choose from, however, you want a **God** choice not a good choice. This prayer allows God to set directions for decisions in your life. You are surrendering to the will of God, not your own will. Jesus had to settle down in prayer and submit his will to God, the Father's will. You must do the same.

Prayer of Thanksgiving, Praise, and Worship:

In these prayers, you are not asking God for things.

Thanksgiving–is thanking God, being grateful, showing gratitude.

Praise–is thanking God for what He has done or what He is getting ready to do.

Worship–is thanking and Praising God for who He is. In worship, your focus is on God.

Prayer Part One

I find an excellent example of these types of prayers in the book of **Acts 16:25-26**.

And at midnight Paul and Silas prayed, and sang praises unto God: and the prisoners heard them. And suddenly there was a great earthquake, so that the foundations of the prison were shaken: and immediately all the doors were opened, and every one's bands were loosed.
—ACTS 16:25-26

They threw Paul and Silas in jail for the sake of the Gospel they preached. Instead of whining and complaining, they prayed and sang praises. I can see them in jail, sitting and reflecting on their situation:

"Because we preached the gospel with such power and demonstration of the Holy Ghost, the churches were strengthened, and the numbers of new converts increased. The hearts and minds of the people were changed because of the good news of the kingdom of God that was proclaimed. As the Holy Spirit displayed His power, even demonic spirits were subject to the name of Jesus. We even cast out a psychic spirit from a woman who was a fortune teller. Her masters got mad and complained to authorities because they could no longer use her to make money."

As they sat there in a dark and dirty cell, reflecting not complaining, I believe a song rose on the inside of them. They sang it aloud on the outside.

The power of their prayer and praise went up to heaven with such a sweet fragrance that God Himself came down to earth to inhabit their praises. The earth shook violently, causing every chain to fall off. The doors that kept them captive flung open.

But thou art holy, O thou that inhabitest the praises of Israel.
—PSALM 22:3

Every man in the prison was set free by the power of God that came down from heaven as our Great God inhabited their praises.

Prayer Part One

Now the Lord is that Spirit: and where the Spirit of the Lord is, there is liberty.
—2 CORINTHIANS 3:17

Sometimes in your life you will have to get up off your knees and stop praying and begin praising. Your praise is a weapon that defeats the enemy every time. When you praise God, you build a throne for him to come down and sit on you. You are not alone; God is with you.

Be careful for nothing; but in everything by prayer and supplication with thanksgiving let your requests be made known unto God.
—PHILIPPIANS 4:6

Notice from the scripture above, you can have petition prayer going on, along with prayers of praise and worship.

Prayer of Intercession:

The word intercession defined is the action of intervention on behalf of another. With this prayer, you are acting in prayer on behalf of someone else. The people you pray for may be incapacitated, out of their mind, under the influence of the devil, drugs, alcohol, or sickness, etc. There may not be anything wrong that you notice. You just want to pray for them.

I exhort therefore, that, first of all, supplications, prayers, intercessions, and giving of thanks, be made for all men; For kings, and for all that are in authority; that we may lead a quiet and peaceable life in all godliness and honesty. For this is good and acceptable in the sight of God our Saviour.
—1 TIMOTHY 2:1-3

You can make prayers of intercession or offer specific prayers based on the knowledge of a person's need. Let us look at Jesus as our intercessor.

For there is one God, and there is one mediator between God and men, the man Christ Jesus...

—1 TIMOTHY 2:5 RSV

Prayer Part One

Jesus is our intercessor before God. In the Old Testament, the priest would stand before God to minister to Him with sacrifices and offerings. He stood between the sinful man and a holy God and brought them together at the place of the blood sacrifice.

The blood in the Old Testament would cover the sins of men. We have a far better intercessor and sacrifice; Jesus, who died on the cross and shed his blood for us. His blood takes away our sins as if we never sinned, instead of just covering our sins. He stands before God interceding on our behalf.

Just as Jesus stands before God on our behalf, we should stand before God on the behalf of others. This is the job and calling of an intercessor. An intercessor is one who takes the place of another or pleads another's case.

Prayer of Binding and Loosing:

Verily I say unto you, Whatsoever ye shall bind on earth shall be bound in heaven: and whatsoever ye shall loose on earth shall be loosed in heaven. Again I say unto you, that if two of you shall agree on earth as touching anything that they shall ask, it shall be done for them of my Father which is in heaven.
—MATTHEW 18:18-19

Bind—*I bind, tie, fasten; I impel, compel;* **I declare to be prohibited and unlawful.** (Strongs Concordance) **To forbid, prohibit, declare to be illicit.** (Thayer's Greek Lexicon) Bind, be in bonds, knit, tie, wind. (Strong's Concordance)

Loose—*Short Definition: I loose,* **untie, release, destroy** *(Strong's Concordance Definition: (a) I loose,* **untie, release.** *(b) met:* **I break, destroy,** *set at naught, contravene; I break up a meeting, annul. 3089 lýō–proper-*

Prayer Part One

*ly, loose **(unleash) let go; release (unbind)** so something no longer holds together; (figuratively) release what has been held back (like Christ "releasing" the seven seals in the scroll in Revelation). (HELPS Word-studies)*

A primary verb: ***to "loosen"*** *(literally or figuratively) —* ***break (up), destroy, dissolve****, (un-) loose, melt, put off. (Strong's Exhaustive Concordance)*

Many people are suffering mentally and or physically by demonic oppression or depression and do not even know it. We can bind demonic spirits that are at work in the lives of people.

We can loose people from the bondages that keep them bound and imprisoned. Binding and loosing are based on the authority God has granted us in his Word. God has given us as believers authority over all devils.

Behold, I have given you authority to tread upon serpents and scorpions, and over all the power of the enemy; and nothing shall hurt you.

—LUKE 10:19 RSV

The word authority used in this verse comes from the Greek word **Exousia**:

Exousía, *ex-oo-see'-ah; from G1832 (in the sense of ability); privilege, i.e.*

(subjectively) force, capacity, competency, freedom,

(objectively) mastery (concretely, magistrate, superhuman, potentate, token of control), delegated influence: authority, jurisdiction, liberty, power, right, strength.

As ambassadors of Christ, we have the **ability, capacity, freedom, jurisdiction, and delegated influence to tread over all the power of the enemy.** We must walk in and use this authority daily. Nothing worse than a person having authority and not knowing how to use it.

Prayer Part One

Jesus has already defeated Satan. We are in the earth to enforce that defeat. We are here in the earth as Ambassadors of the Kingdom of Heaven. It is our duty to display the Kingdom of Heaven in the earth. We must use the authority that God has given us to set the captives free.

Now, with binding and loosing, one simple way of understanding these types of prayers are the two words. To "bind" which means to forbid. To "lose" which means to permit. These were common terms used by Jewish scholars in the bible. I like the following translation of Matthew 18:18:

I solemnly say to you, whatever you forbid on earth must be already forbidden in heaven, and whatever you permit on earth must be already permitted in heaven."
—MATTHEW 18:18 CWT

In this translation, you see the clarity of what Jesus wants you to do as a believer. He wants you to use your authority that He has given you to allow, permit, or forbid certain activities. Later in the book of John, after the disciples receive the Holy Spirit, Jesus tells them:

> *Whosoever sins ye remit, they are remitted unto them; and whosoever sins ye retain, they are retained.*
> —JOHN 20:23

In John 20:23 you see the words binding and loosing as remit and retain (keep) which is permitting and forbidding. This is what we must do in prayer as believers when certain situations arise, we must use our authority over the situation. Remember, Jesus gave us authority in the first chapter of Ephesians. It reads:

> *[15] That's why, when I heard of the solid trust you have in the Master Jesus and your outpouring of love to all the followers of Jesus, [16] I couldn't stop thanking God for you—every time I prayed, I'd think of you and give thanks.*
>
> *[17] But I do more than thank. I ask—ask the God of our Master, Jesus Christ, the God of glory—to*

make you intelligent and discerning in knowing him personally, [18]*your eyes focused and clear, so that you can see exactly what it is he is calling you to do, grasp the immensity of this glorious way of life he has for his followers,*

[19]*oh, the utter extravagance of his work in us who trust him—endless energy, boundless strength!* [20]*All this energy issues from Christ: God raised him from death and set him on a throne in deep heaven,*

[21]*in charge of running the universe, everything from galaxies to governments, no name and no power exempt from his rule. And not just for the time being, but forever.*

[22]*He is in charge of it all, has the final word on everything.* <u>*At the center of all this, Christ rules the church.*</u> [23]<u>*The church, you see, is not peripheral to the world; the world is peripheral to the church. The church is Christ's body, in which he speaks and acts, by which he fills everything with his presence.*</u>

—EPHESIANS 1:15-23 MSG

Jesus is in charge and we are His body. We are attached together in Him. Since Jesus is seated in deep heaven at the right hand of God, the seat of authority, we are seated in deep heaven at the right hand of God with Him.

This is the seat we rule from as the body of Christ. God's authority rules over all the power of the enemy, and nothing by any means shall hurt us.

Chapter Five

Prayer Part 2

Praying In The Spirit And With The Understanding

Now that we have seen the different types of prayers, we need to look at the two ways of praying. Praying in the spirit (tongues) and praying with the understanding (your known language).

> *But whosoever drinketh of the water that I shall give him shall never thirst; but the water that I shall give him shall be in him a well of water springing up into everlasting life.*
> —JOHN 4:14

The well of water in the passage represents the Holy Spirit living on the **inside** of the believer once a person receives salvation. He comes on the inside and works from the inside out. He is forever flowing, never ending, and releases everlasting life into the believer.

He brings with him the fruit of the Spirit, which are the Holy Spirit's attributes. Attributes are characteristic ascribed to someone or something.

The Holy Spirit's attributes are in the following verse:

But the fruit of the Spirit is love, joy, peace, longsuffering, gentleness, goodness, faith, Meekness, temperance: against such there is no law.

–GALATIANS 5:22-23

The fruit of the Holy Spirit flows out of you from the inside as you yield and submit your life to the Word of God and the prompting of the Holy Spirit. This blesses you from the inside and

Prayer Part 2

makes you a better person. The second work of the Holy Spirit is **upon** you. The word "upon" means "up and on."

> *But ye shall receive power, after that the Holy Ghost is <u>come upon you</u>: and ye shall be witnesses unto me both in Jerusalem, and in all Judaea, and in Samaria, and unto the uttermost part of the earth.*
> —ACTS 1:8

God wants the Holy Spirit to come up from the well on the inside of you and get on you. The first example of this is in Acts 2.

> *[1]And when the day of Pentecost was fully come, they were all with one accord in one place. [2]And suddenly there came a sound from heaven as of a rushing mighty wind, and it filled all the house where they were sitting. [3]And there appeared unto them cloven tongues like as of fire, and it sat <u>upon</u> each of them. [4]And they were all filled with the Holy Ghost, and began to speak with other tongues, as the Spirit gave them utterance.*
> —ACTS 2:1-4

The Holy Spirit gave them utterance. When you have the infilling of the Holy Spirit, He gives you the ability to speak in an unknown tongue. The Holy Spirit will not make you speak; however, you must cooperate with Him and open your mouth and do the speaking by faith.

The Holy Spirit will give you the utterance, but you are the one that must speak it out. Once you are filled with the Holy Spirit and begin speaking in tongues, you now have a new tongue (unknown to you) prayer language, that the enemy cannot stop.

Tongues is available to every person who is born again and **believes**.

And these signs follow them that believe; In my name shall they cast out devils; <u>they shall speak with new tongues</u>; They shall take up serpents; and if they drink any deadly thing, it shall not hurt them; they shall lay hands on the sick, and they shall recover.
                              —MARK 16:17-18

Prayer Part 2

This is a sign to those who believe. If you want the Holy Spirit to come upon you (to be filled with the Holy Ghost is how we say it in the church world), ask God to fill you with the Holy Spirit.

> *[11] If a son shall ask bread of any of you that is a father, will he give him a stone? Or if he ask a fish, will he for a fish give him a serpent?*
>
> *[12] Or if he shall ask an egg, will he offer him a scorpion? [13] If ye then, being evil, know how to give good gifts unto your children: how much more shall your heavenly Father give the Holy Spirit to them that ask him?*
>
> —LUKE 11:11-13

Once you ask God, He will fill you. You must start the speaking, and the Holy Spirit will give you the utterance in another tongue.

The third work of the Holy Spirit is the work of Him **flowing out of you**. Let us look at this translation from John chapter 7:

> *[37] Now on the final and most important day of the*

Feast, Jesus stood, and He cried in a loud voice, If any man is thirsty, let him come to Me and drink!

[38] He who believes in Me [who cleaves to and trusts in and relies on Me] as the Scripture has said, From his innermost being shall flow [continuously] <u>springs and rivers of living water</u>.

[39] But He was speaking here of the Spirit, Whom those who believed (trusted, had faith) in Him were afterward to receive. For the [Holy] Spirit had not yet been given, because Jesus was not yet glorified (raised to honor).
—JOHN 7:37-39 AMPC

Remember, once the Holy Spirit enters you, you can have living waters flowing out of you. The verse above talks about springs and rivers. Let us look at the differences in the two:

Spring— *is water that flows* <u>**up from under the ground**</u> *and forms small stream, or pools.* (Macmillan online dictionary)

Prayer Part 2

But there went up a mist from the earth and watered the whole face of the ground. And the Lord <u>God formed man of the dust of the ground</u> and breathed into his nostrils the breath of life; and man became a living soul.

—GENESIS 2:6-8

Did you catch that? Springs comes from the ground. God still has water flowing out of the ground; **man**, which is made from the dust of the ground.

River—*a large area of water that flows toward the ocean.* (Macmillan online dictionary)

A River and a Stream are both fast moving bodies of water, but a river is called a River because it is larger, deeper, and longer than a stream. As for a stream, it is much less than a river but not as deep. You can even walk across it. Another difference is that a stream is a small flowing water. And a river is a collection of many streams. (Forest and Stream Sportsmen's Encyclopedia, Volume 62 pg. 276)

Many streams of the Holy Spirit come together and flow on the inside of you. They turn into rivers of living water on the inside of you to flow and bless the oceans of people on the outside of you. Here is the other translation of the verse in the book of John that I like:

37 On the final and climactic day of the Feast, Jesus took his stand. He cried out, "If anyone thirsts, let him come to me and drink.

38 Rivers of living water will brim and spill out of the depths of anyone who believes in me this way, just as the Scripture says."

39 (He said this in regard to the Spirit, whom those who believed in him were about to receive. The Spirit had not yet been given because Jesus had not yet been glorified).
—JOHN 7:37-39 MSG

Do not end up being a Christian that is **filled** with God's power, but not **spilled** with God's power. Don't be so stingy with the power of God that you have an island mentality with your

Prayer Part 2

born-again experience. Remember, the purpose of the Holy Spirit was to endue you with power to be a witness.

> *Behold, I send the Promise of My Father upon you; but tarry in the city [a]of Jerusalem until you are endued with power from on high."*
> —LUKE 24:48 NKJV

> *But you shall receive power (ability, efficiency, and might) when the Holy Spirit has come upon you, and you shall be My witnesses in Jerusalem and all Judea and Samaria and to the ends (the very bounds) of the earth.*
> —ACTS 1:8 AMPC

Once you have the power of God flowing out of you, it is time to be a witness. It starts by letting the Fruit of the Spirit work in you. The Fruit of the Spirit are the attributes of the Holy Spirit that you must yield to as He works on the inside of you to make you more like God.

At the same time, it is praying in the Spirit so you can become more sensitive to the ways of the

Spirit of God. One benefit of praying in the Spirit is that it charges you up like a battery.

But you, my friends, keep on building yourselves up on your most sacred faith. Pray in the power of the Holy Spirit.
—JUDE 20 GNT

But you, beloved, build yourselves up on [the foundation of] your most holy faith [continually progress, rise like an edifice higher and higher], pray in the Holy Spirit.
—JUDE 20 AMP

The more time you spend in praying in the Spirit, the more you will begin moving in the power of the Spirit. You will be a light in the darkness and the Holy Spirit will teach you how to flow with Him as you spend more time in prayer and the Word of God.

PRAYING WITH THE UNDERSTANDING

Praying with the understanding is praying in your own known language. This is you using the

Prayer Part 2

Word of God with the right prayer, for the situation you are praying for. Now that you know the types of prayers and the two ways you can pray. Pray! Pray! Pray! Your prayers will be different daily but be open to flowing with the Spirit of God. If you do not know what to pray in your language, pray in tongues.

Likewise, the Spirit also helpeth our infirmities: for we know not what we should pray for as we ought: but the Spirit itself [Himself] maketh intercession for us with groanings which cannot be uttered. ²⁷And he that searcheth the hearts knoweth what is the mind of the Spirit, because he maketh intercession for the saints according to the will of God.
—ROMANS 8:26-27

Notice the Holy Spirit intercedes for the saints according to the will of God. The Holy Spirit will help you pray the will of God in tongues. Your natural mind will not understand it. That is ok, the will of God is being prayed and that is what counts.

ALL THINGS WORKING TOGETHER

Now many in the church world can quote the scripture:

And we know that all things work together for good to them that love God, to them who are the called according to his purpose.

—**ROMANS 8:28 KJV**

Some take this verse out of context to mean that everything that happens in their life, good or bad, God is working it out for their good. They lose their job; They say "all things are working for my good." The death of a loved one in a tragic accident; they say it is working for my good. That is far from the truth.

Let's look at the verse more in context:

[26]Likewise the Spirit also helpeth our infirmities: for we know not what we should pray for as we ought: but the Spirit itself maketh intercession for us with groanings which cannot be uttered.

Prayer Part 2

²⁷And he that searcheth the hearts knoweth what is the mind of the Spirit, because he maketh intercession for the saints according to the will of God.

²⁸And we know that all things work together for good to them that love God, to them who are the called according to his purpose.

—ROMANS 8:26-28

Therefore, when you look at the verse in context, all things work together is referring to all things of prayer, not all things that happen in your life, good or bad. Now we learned in 1 Corinthians:

What is it then? I will pray with the spirit, and I will pray with the understanding also: I will sing with the spirit, and I will sing with the understanding also.

—1 CORINTHIANS 14:15

Let us bring it all together with clarity and understanding. To maximize your praying, pray in the spirit and with the understanding together.

Let me explain this, whatever situation you are praying about, there are some things you know and some things you do not know. How do you pray this out? Start by praying what you know, when you get to where you do not know what to pray, pray in tongues. Now here is the important part.

Wherefore let him that speaketh in an unknown tongue pray that he may interpret.
—1 CORINTHIANS 14:13

After praying in tongues for a few minutes, ask the Lord for the interpretation. Then speak out in your own language what comes to you immediately. Write it down and when the flow stops, pray in the spirit again. Stop. Speak out the first thing that comes to you. Write it down and repeat this process. The more you do this, the easier it becomes to distinguish what is being prayed out in the Spirit.

One way you can distinguish if what you are saying is from God is that it will line up com-

Prayer Part 2

pletely with His Word. I have done this for many years. Recently I connected and understood how to do this, praying things out effectively, working with the Holy Spirit.

As a music minister and singer, I played the keyboard and sung. I would begin by worshiping and singing in tongues, yielding to the Holy Spirit. Afterwards I gave the interpretation or flowed prophetically in English. The Holy Spirit pulled things out of my heart that I could not express in my known language. I sang in the spirit, and the Holy Spirit would take hold together with my spirit to help my infirmities.

Infirmities– *an unsound or unhealthy state of body; weakness of mind; weakness of resolution.*

The Holy Spirit helped me pray the perfect will of God for my life. As I sang in the spirit, then I would prophesy in a known language that which was in the mind of the Spirit.

As I was chasing the Lord with hunger. I would go to my garage to pray in tongues. I would stop and ask the Lord for the interpretation. He would give it to me immediately. I practiced this in private, so I would be a yielded vessel, able to flow with the Holy Spirit in a corporate setting.

Many times, when the gifts of the spirit are in operation, many would recognize the move of the Spirit, but not know how to flow with Him. The Gift of Tongues would manifest; however, no one would give the interpretation or recognize that it manifested.

The only way I can explain it is that it differs from praying in tongues in your prayer language. When you pray in tongues, you control and start speaking in tongues as you will. This tongue is from earth to Heaven. When the Gift of tongues is in operation, this tongue comes from heaven down. It is the Holy Spirit speaking to you from heaven.

Prayer Part 2

In my experience, I recognized it two ways. First, when someone else begins speaks with the Gift of tongues, there is a shift in what you hear, and it is only spiritually discerned. Second, when I pray in tongues and there is a shift, I recognize on the inside that this is coming from heaven down. I pray it out and ask for the interpretation.

Now in saying all that, I practiced asking the Lord for the interpretation during my private prayer time so when I was in a corporate setting, I was ready and willing to flow. When I recognized the manifestation of the Gift of tongues, I would pray for the interpretation and flow with the Spirit of God giving the interpretation. There are a lot of believers that have not learned how to flow with the Spirit.

They would hear the interpretation, but not speak it out loud because they were afraid. They were afraid of making a mistake or being out of order in a church setting. I would ask the Lord for the interpretation and speak it out so that all could be edified.

When you bring all these things together when praying, using the right tool at the right time, you now pray more effectively and with powerful results.

Chapter Six

Listen

Life is full of many stimulations: television, cell phones, computers, and social media. Everything is pulling at you. The world system has you busy and distracted. Countless people pray to God, however, they are the only ones doing the talking. Many have been taught to pray to God, however, they have not been trained to sit and listen for God's response. You want to have a conversation with God, but maybe you forgot what a conversation means.

Conversation – *is an informal, usually private, talk in which two or more people exchange thoughts, feelings, or ideas, or in which news or* *information is given or discussed* (Cambridge Dictionaries Online).

It takes two or more to have a conversation. Learn to listen when you are praying, which is having a conversation with God. He hears you when you pray, but do you hear Him? You must be **still** enough to let Him speak to you. The Bible encourages us in Psalm 46:

> *Be still and know that I am God: I will be exalted among the heathen, I will be exalted in the earth.*
> —PSALM 46:10

"Be still and know that I am God..." We must learn how to settle ourselves down and get into a quiet place. Find an area, somewhere where you can spend some quiet time with the Lord. It may be a closet, a study, back porch, bedroom, or garage. Find somewhere where you and the Lord can meet. Shut off your cell phone. Remove every distraction and seek the Lord. Schedule a daily time for you and the Lord to meet.

Listen

Be prompt. Go in with expectation, let nothing get between you and your time with the Lord. Once you are there, open your heart to hear His voice.

My sheep hear my voice, and I know them, and they follow me:
—JOHN 10:27

As you sit in the presence of God, listen for His voice. Listen defined by Webster's Dictionary is:

Listen–*to pay attention to someone or something in order to hear what is being said, sung, played, etc. To hear what someone has said and understand that it is serious, important, or true.*

During your prayer, take time to listen to what God is saying to you. One challenge you may have when you pray is distinguishing God's voice. You may sit there in prayer saying to yourself, "is that me or is that God talking? Is it just my mind playing tricks on me, saying things I want to hear?" You are unsure of what you are hearing in your head. Remember, Jesus said:

> *"The sheep that are My own hear and are listening to My voice; and I know them, and they follow Me."*
>
> —JOHN 10:27

God is talking to you. You must learn how to tune into His voice. There are many voices out there. How do you know when God is speaking? First, when God is speaking, what is being said ALWAYS lines up with the Word of God. God says nothing that does not line up with His Word. I do not care what you think you heard, felt, or saw, God will say nothing that does not fall in line with His Word.

Second, I encourage you to get a journal. Begin writing everything you hear when you are in the presence of God. Even if you think it is your mind talking. Just write what you believe is being said. Put a date and time on it. Now you have a reference point in your journal.

Listen

What God will do is confirm His Word. He will tell you things and they will come to pass. As God continues to reveal things to you, your journal will be a written documentation that you were hearing from God. As you spend that quiet time with God writing what you are hearing, you are fine tuning your hearing. After a while, you learn to distinguish and know God's voice. You confirm what you heard with the Written Word of God.

I practiced this myself. Then I notice how my prayer life changed. I heard and recognized God's voice more clearly. I gained more confidence because I can distinguish His voice over all the clutter in my mind. He keeps on confirming His Word. My journals prove it repeatedly.

Here is a caution. If there is something you are desiring badly, take extra time to make sure you are hearing God's voice and not your own desires. The key is looking at our example of Jesus when He was in the Garden of Gethsemane.

36 Then Jesus went with them to a place called Gethsemane, and He told His disciples, Sit down here while I go over yonder and pray. 37 And taking with Him Peter and the two sons of Zebedee, He began to [a] show grief and distress of mind and was [b]deeply depressed.

38 Then He said to them, My soul is very sad and deeply grieved, so that [c]I am almost dying of sorrow. Stay here and keep awake and keep watch with Me.

39 And going a little farther, He threw Himself upon the ground on His face and prayed saying, My Father, if it is possible, let this cup pass away from Me; nevertheless, not what I will [not what I desire], but as You will and desire.

—MATTHEW 26:36-46 AMP

If there was another way for Jesus not to have to experience the crucifixion, He Himself would have taken it. But the key is in verse thirty-nine, **(nevertheless, not what I will [not what I desire], but as You will and desire).** He laid

Listen

down his **will** and **desire** and instead **yielded to the will of God the Father**. Wow, what an example for us to follow!

We must keep our will and desires surrendered to the will of God the Father. God is speaking to us in these last days. Are you willing to hear and obey? Hearing and obeying will change your life forever. God is looking for those of us who want His plan and purpose in our lives.

He wants to make an enormous impact on the earth. All He needs is a few good men who will hear and obey what He says and do it.

Chapter Seven

Confessions

Many in the body of Christ have an identity crisis. They really do not know who they are in Christ. Once you are born again, you are a new creation. When you get the revelation of who you are and what happened to you, you would act differently, walk differently, and your conversation would change. You would walk and live victoriously in every area of your life.

It's like when a child is adopted into a new family. He takes on the new family's name and has all the legal rights and privileges that come with being a part of the new family. The child becomes a joint heir with the other children. The moment you **confess with your mouth Jesus is Lord and believe in your heart that God has raised Him from the dead, you are born again** into a new family. You are now one of God's children. You are joint heirs with Jesus.

Let us look closer at being a joint heir. If you have a joint bank account, that is a shared account with someone else. Whoever's name is on the account has full access to everything that is in the account. You are joint heirs with Jesus. The bible says He is the firstborn among many brethren.

For whom he did foreknow, he also did predestinate to be conformed to the image of his Son, that he might be the firstborn among many brethren.
—ROMANS 8:29

Who do you think are the brethren? Those of us who are born again. Because we are born again, we now have full access to everything that Jesus has access to. Why? Because we are children of God. Wow, this is powerful when you think about

Confessions

it! What did Jesus have access to? Signs, wonders, and miracles. He healed the sick, raised the dead, spoke to storms, walked on water, multiplied food, etc. These are things in our account in heaven that will manifest in the earth once we learn how to access our heavenly accounts.

Once you are born again, you are born into a new family. The new family is the family of God. Jesus is the first-born son of our family. He is our older brother. It is imperative that we change the way we see ourselves. How do we do this? Let us look to the Word of God for the answer.

> ***My heart is inditing a good matter: I speak of the things which I have made touching the king: <u>my tongue is the pen of a ready writer.</u>***
> —PSALM 45:1

We must use our spoken words more intentionally. Using our spoken words is the key to changing how we see ourselves. The words we speak have the power to change, rearrange and create things. Let me put it to you this way, **"WORDS"** are image containers. These image containers work like seeds.

Speaking a Word out of your mouth produces an image. Where you find yourself in life today, is a result from the words you have spoken out of your mouth yesterday. If you dislike where you are today **MAKE A CHANGE** in what you are saying. Begin confessing today to create your tomorrow.

Now just like a seed, when you plant it in the ground, the ground breaks it down, and the seed grows into the plant that it is programmed in the seed to produce. Your words are spiritual seeds. The plan of salvation is a spiritual seed.

In becoming born again, you had to **confess with your mouth** and **believe in your heart**. Confessing with your mouth and believing in your heart is not just for your salvation, it is a formula for making the Word of God alive in your life.

Confessions

The word "confess" comes from a primary Greek word "homologeo", which means "to say the same thing and then agree, admit, acknowledge." You need to confess (say the same thing and then agree, admit, and acknowledge) the Word of God over your life. Say the same thing the bible says about you. Here are some examples:

For God hath not given us the spirit of fear; but of power, and of love, and of a sound mind.
—2 TIMOTHY 1:7

Confession—God has not given me the spirit of fear, but of power and of love, and a sound mind.

I can do all things through Christ which strengtheneth me. —PHILIPPIANS 4:13

Confession—I can do all things through Christ who strengthens me.

I shall not die, but live, and declare the works of the LORD. —PSALM 118:17

Confession–I shall not die, but live, and declare the works of the Lord.

Ye are of God, little children, and have overcome them: because greater is he that is in you, than he that is in the world. —1 JOHN 4:4

Confession–Greater is he that is within me, than he that is in the world.

These are a few examples of things you can confess out of your mouth, out loud, over your life.

Jesus died so that the New Testament could go into effect. Then he rose again to make sure everything that he said would not only come to pass but be enforced. All we must do is **read** the will, **speak** the will, **believe** the will, and **receive** the will. The will is the Word of God.

IMAGINATION

As I stated before, the words we speak produce images. We see those images on the canvas of our imagination. The imagination, or the way I like to put it, **"Image Nation,"** is a powerful, creative place. When you speak words out of your mouth, the word **(image containers)** carry those word images to the canvas of your imagination. It paints a picture in your mind of whatever that word image is.

The word containers that produce the images you see on the canvas of your imagination are influenced by what you have been taught, thought, or believe by internal recollections and/or external sensations gathered by your five senses. Your imagination is like a creative lab. In that lab you can manipulate, transform, rearrange, or create anything you can conceive possible. The imagination is so powerful that you can experience things so vividly which can affect your reality. Your imagination can influence your perception.

Here is an example: I want you to imagine in your mind, a big yellow lemon. Now imagine taking a knife and cutting the lemon in half. Imagine you smell the tartness of the lemon. Now squeeze the lemon juice into your mouth to where the juice touches your tongue and fills your mouth.

Notice as you are imagining this, your saliva glands salivate as you've only imagined tasting the lemon juice in your mouth. If you use your imagination as a lab to create a blueprint of who you are in Christ, using the Word of God as your material to create the image, you will see yourself the way God sees you.

The more you fill your imagination with Gods Word, the clearer the picture becomes. Then it manifests from the spirit realm to the natural realm and becomes your reality.

Confessions

Imagination–*the act or power of forming a mental image of something not present to the senses or never before wholly perceived in reality.* (Merriam-Webster online dictionary)

As you confess the Word of God daily, you now go from just living life any kind of way to orchestrating and designing your life the way God wants you to live.

You are now becoming kingdom minded and beginning to act the way children of the kingdom of God act. You rule in life the way God wanted you to rule in life from the beginning.

For whom he did foreknow, he also did predestinate to be conformed to the image of his Son, that he might be the firstborn among many brethren.
—ROMANS 8:29

As you continue to confess the Word of God over your life daily. You now conform to the image of Christ. Paul said it like this:

"My little children, of whom I travail in birth

again until Christ be formed in you,"
—GALATIANS 4:19

Declare God's Word over your life and watch the Word of God change you from the inside out.

MEDITATION

Another especially important part of confession is meditation. When I first saw the word meditation, I never saw it in its fulness. I pictured a monk sitting in a temple with his legs crossed and eyes closed, humming. Now when I investigated the Word of God and saw the word meditate in the book of Joshua, I knew there was something that I was missing.

This book of the law shall not depart out of thy mouth; but thou shalt meditate therein day and night, that thou mayest observe to do according to all that is written therein: for then thou shalt make thy way prosperous, and then thou shalt have good success.
—JOSHUA 1:8

Confessions

I wanted good success, so I needed to know what it means to meditate. The word meditate in the above verse comes from the Hebrew word hagah. (pronounced daw-gaw') The KJV translates Strong's H1897 (Hagah) in the following-manner: meditate, to ponder, imagine, mourn, mutter, roar, X sore, speak, study, talk, utter.

As I looked at the words above, words like mutter, roar, speak, talk, the word utter popped out to me. I always thought meditation was just sitting silently, however, as I looked up the Hebrew word for meditate, there was more happening than me just sitting in silence thinking. Then I looked up the word meditate in the dictionary; here is what I discovered:

Meditate–*to engage in contemplation or reflection to focus one's thoughts on, reflect on or ponder over to plan or project in the mind, intend, purpose.* (Merriam-Webster online dictionary)

Here is where I started seeing more clearly what God wants us to do when we meditate:

Ponder: *to weigh in the mind, to think about, reflect on.*

Imagine: *to form a mental image of (something not present) archaic: plan, scheme.*

Mutter: *to utter sounds or words indistinctly or with a low voice and with the lips partly closed.*

Speak: *to utter words or articulate sounds with the ordinary voice: talk.*

Meditation is more than just thinking about something; it also involves muttering and speaking. That makes sense to me. When I speak a thing out of my mouth, it produces an image. That image is painted on the canvas of my imagination.

Now that I have an image of that thing, as I continue to speak it out of my mouth, it fills the canvas of my imagination with clarity. I now see the correlation of meditation and faith. The bible says: ***So then faith cometh by hearing, and hearing by the word of God.*** —ROMANS 10:17

Confessions

When you are meditating (muttering, speaking) the Word of God, you are hearing it in your ear, but seeing it in your imagination.

Now faith is the substance of things hoped for, the evidence of things not seen.
—HEBREWS 11:1

Faith is the material of the things hoped for. Faith is equal to the phrase "Word of God" in some places in the bible.

If this statement is true, I can insert the phrase "Word of God" in some places where I see the word "Faith" and it will not change the meaning of the scripture but illuminate it even more. Let's try it.

Now faith is the substance of things hoped for, the evidence of things not seen.
—HEBREWS 11:1

Now the **Word of God** is the substance of things hoped for, the evidence of things not seen.

Now the just shall live by faith: but if any man draw back, my soul shall have no pleasure in him.
—HEBREWS 10:38

Now the just shall live by the **Word of God**: but if any man draw back, my soul shall have no pleasure in him.

For we walk by faith, not by sight.
—2 CORINTHIANS 5:7

For I walk by **The Word Of God** and not by sight.

You can now see the importance of meditating on the **Word of God.** For you to have faith, you must hear it. What better way to hear the Word of God than out of your own mouth as you are meditating on it. Faith is vital to you as a believer. The bible says:

For therein is the righteousness of God revealed from faith to faith: as it is written, The just shall live by faith. —ROMANS 1:17

Confessions

I like to think of it like this; if you are not living by faith, you are not living, you are existing. As a believer, God commands us to live by faith. The way we receive faith is by hearing the Word of God. We must hear the Word of God repeatedly to increase our faith. One of the best ways to hear the Word of God is by you speaking it out of your own mouth.

Chapter Eight

Worship

Whatis worship? Worship comes from an Old English word *"worðscip."*

wurðscip (Anglian)

weorðscipe (West Saxon)
condition of being worthy, dignity, glory, distinction, honor, renown

weorð
"worthy" (see worth) + -scpe (see ship) worth (adj.)

weorþ
(Old English) significant, valuable, of value; valued, appreciated, highly thought of,

deserving, meriting; honorable, noble, of high rank; suitable for, proper, fit, capable-ship

Word-forming element meaning quality, condition; act, power, skill; office, position; relation between

As we look at the English Word for worship, it seems to not give us a clear picture of what worship is. To truly define Worship, you realize it is an attitude and an act.

In the Bible, you see the word worship in the old and in the New Testament. The word translated worship in our language has different meanings in the Hebrew and Greek languages. There are unique words used to describe worship.

This set of Greek and Hebrew words gives us the **proper viewpoint** we need to have toward God:

–Greek words **sebo** and **eusebeo** derived from **sebas** - *"fear or reverence"*.

–Hebrew word **yârê'** (yaw-ray) and **yir'âh**

Worship

(yir-aw) in Greek, **phobeõ** *(fob-eh'-o) or* **Phobos** *(fob'-os)–"to fear; morally to revere; dreadful exceeding fearfulness; reverence to be in awe; in terror."*

This set of Greek and Hebrew words gives us the **proper position** we have toward God:

–Hebrew word **shachah** *- "bowing down before an object of honor."*

–Hebrew word **segid** *- "showing respect," or "doing homage."*

–Greek words **gonu** *and* **gonupeteo** *- "bending the knee."*

–Greek word **proskuneo***, derived from* **pros***, "toward" and* **kuneo***, "to kiss."*

This set of Greek and Hebrew words gives us the **proper result** that we have when worshiping God:

–Hebrew word **abad** *- "service or work for God."*

–*Greek word **latreuo**, derived from **latris** "servant."*

–*Greek word **leitourgeo**, derived from **laos**, "people", and **ergeo**, "to work.".*

–*Greek word **therapeuo** - «to heal.»*

When we tie all of this together, we see worship involving proper viewpoint, proper position, and the proper results. Worship is first seeing God right. Seeing He has value and is worthy of our praise is the viewpoint you must have.

Next is a proper position: Proper position is having the right attitude toward God. That attitude is reverence. Having the right attitude toward God will cause us to have the proper result, which causes us to act properly.

One act that we do is to bow down to reverence Him. We must serve Him with all our hearts. We must give Him the honor for who He is. Praise thanks God for what He has done; Worship gives thanks to God for who He is.

Worship

Take a moment now and just Worship God. Bow down, open your heart, say this prayer, and love on Him. He is an awesome God!

Lord, we love You today. We bow our heads to You. We surrender our hearts to You. We reverence and invite Your holy presence in as You enter the room. We are grateful for Your love, Your tender mercies. We acknowledge Your presence even now as many are reading this book. Your presence, Your essence is flowing from the pages into their hearts. Lord fill us up with more of Your love, with more of Your glory, with more of Your power. Break every shackle of our minds and give us understanding. We seek You with all our heart, with all our mind, and all our passion. Take control of our lives and live through us. We love you. Thank You for sending Your son for our sake. Have Your way in our lives from this day forth, in Jesus' Name Amen!!

CONCLUSION

So, are you busy with life? Here is a strategy to help incorporate prayer in your life. Begin breaking down your prayer time to increments of 5-minute slots throughout your day or all at once. Do not be so rigid on five minutes back-to-back. Be flexible, but intentional daily on making time for God through prayer.

Take five minutes a day on each of the steps on the next page. Watch your life transition to a better version of yourself.

Now if you get stuck on one part longer than five minutes, go with the flow. It is not always important to hit every step all the time. It is important that you are **MAKING A Change** and MAKING time for God.

Conclusion

Freshen Up—confess your sins to God

Praise—Praise God for what he has done and is about to do.

Read—Read the Word of God daily

Pray—Pray the Word of God. Pray with the understanding and in tongues.

Listen—STOP! Settle down and listen to what the Lord is saying and WRITE it down.

Confessions—Confess the promises of God over your life and change the image of the World to the image of the Word in your imagination.

Worship—Thank and reverence God for who He is.

Prayer of Salvation

Here is one of the best parts of the book; leading you to salvation. When I say the word salvation, you might have heard other terms such as being born again, saved, and a few others. You may wonder if you are saved. Here is a simple question to ask yourself. If you were to die today, where would you spend eternity, heaven, or hell? If you cannot say 100% that you know you would end up in heaven, you may not be born again. Here is the simple solution.

Speak the prayer on the next page, out loud with your mouth, and believe in your heart, and you will be born again. The Word of God gives us a formula in the book of Romans.

because, if you confess with your lips that Jesus is Lord and believe in your heart that God raised him from the dead, you will be saved. For man believes with his heart and so is justified, and he confesses with his lips and so is saved.

—ROMANS 10:9-10 RSV

PRAYER OF SALVATION

God, please forgive me for everything I have done or said that was not pleasing in your sight. I make a decision to turn away from sin and turn to you. Father Your Word says, if I confess with my mouth that Jesus is Lord and believe in my heart that you raised Jesus from the dead, I will be saved. Today I am making this decision. Father, I confess with my mouth that Jesus is Lord; I believe in my heart that You raised Jesus from the dead. Now, according to your Word, I am saved. Thank You for saving me.

CONGRATULATIONS!!

Welcome to the family. God has never been hard to work with. He was just waiting for you to come home. Being saved does not mean you are going to be perfect. You still may make mistakes, but God has given us a way to get clean again.

If we confess our sins, he is faithful and just, and will forgive our sins and cleanse us from all unrighteousness.
—1 JOHN 1:9

Just confess your sins before God; He will forgive you and wash you clean. Next, forgive yourself and move on.

Prayer for Baptism of the Holy Spirit

Now that you are born again, the Holy Spirit came on the inside of you and made a new you in you. The work of the Holy Spirit in your life is not complete, however, He wants to come upon you. The word "upon" means "up and on."

The only qualification to receiving the baptism of the Holy Spirit, is that you must be born again. To receive the Baptism of the Holy Spirit with the evidence of speaking in tongues, all we must do is ask God in faith.

[10] For everyone who asks receives, and he who seeks finds, and to him who knocks it will be opened. [11] If a son asks for bread from any father among you, will he give him a stone? Or if he asks for a fish, will he give him a serpent instead of a fish? [12] Or if he asks for an egg, will he offer him a scorpion? [13] If you then, being evil, know

Prayer for the Baptism of the Holy Spirit

---

how to give good gifts to your children, how much more will your heavenly Father give the Holy Spirit to those who ask Him!

—LUKE 11:10-13 NKJV

If you need a **point of contact** to release your faith, lay your hand on my handprint on the page 143. As you lay your hand on the handprint, the power of God will come upon you mightily. I have released the anointing of God upon these books for the baptism of the Holy Spirit, healing, and deliverance.

PRAYER TO RECEIVE THE BAPTISM OF THE HOLY SPIRIT

Father God, I come to you asking to receive the baptism of the Holy Spirit with the evidence of speaking in tongues. Your Word says you will give the Holy Spirit to them that asks you. I ask now by faith that you fill me up with your Holy Spirit, let him come up and on me in Jesus' Name! I now believe that I have received him. Thank you for filling me, Amen!!

The next step is to begin speaking in tongues. The Holy Spirit will not force you to do it, you must step out in faith and just do it. Here is how you are going to do it. Simple, open your mouth and begin speaking. Do not just open your mouth and think it is automatic. YOU must begin speaking.

Take a deep breath and begin to speak. It may be a syllable or two, it may sound like baby talk. Just let Him flow. The more you let Him flow, the easier it will become.

Point of Contact

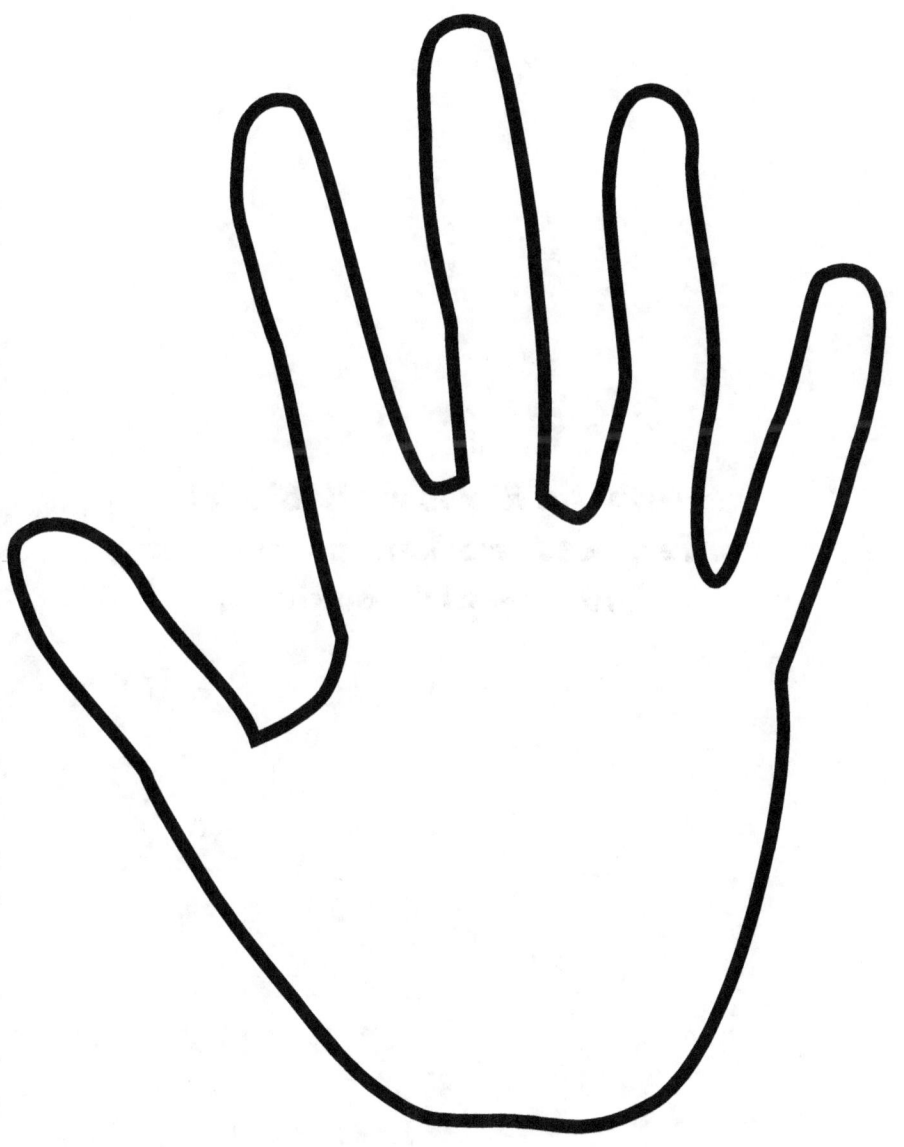

Apostle Ray is available for conferences, workshops, seminars, and ministry bookings.

machangepublisher@gmail.com

Apostle Darrell Ray

Apostle Darrell Ray is a messenger of God's Word who operates in revelation and activation. He is an author, business consultant, conference speaker, and a high-impact teacher. His teachings enable the Body of Christ to see and understand the truth of the scriptures with simplicity. He is the founder of Make A Change Ministries and Darrell Ray Ministries. He is married to Crystalline and they have four daughters and seven grandchildren.

**CONTACT INFORMATION FOR
APOSTLE DARRELL R. RAY
Email: apostledarrellray@gmail.com
Facebook: apostledarrellray**

**For a complete list of our titles
visit us at www.changepublishers.com.**

machangepublisher@gmail.com

Books Available Now

Expelling The Beast From Within
by Crystalline Ray

Psalms 119 A Call To Holiness
by Crystalline Ray, Darrell Ray,
Jerome Sparks

Psalms 119 Wisdom Keys Journal
by Crystalline Ray, Darrell Ray,
Jerome Sparks

Coming Soon

Psalms 119 Wisdom Keys
by Crystalline Ray, Darrell Ray,
Jerome Sparks

CHANGE PUBLISHERS

Columbia, South Carolina

BIBLE TRANSLATIONS

Abbreviation	Name	Publication Date
AMP	The Amplified Bible	1964 (NT - 1958; Revised 1987)
AMPC	Amplified Bible, Classic Edition	1987
ASV	American Standard Version	1901
KJV AV	King James Version (also known as Authorized Version)	1611
LIV	The Living Bible	1971 (NT - 1962)
MSG	The Message (New Testament only)	1993
NASB	New American Standard Bible (NASB)	1971 (NT - 1963; Revised 1996)
NIV	New International Version	1978 (NT - 1973)
NKJV	New King James Version	1982
NLT	New Living Translation	1996
NRSV	New Revised Standard Version	1990
RSV	Revised Standard Version	1952 (NT - 1946; NT revised 1971)
TPT	The Passion Translation	
WIL	Williams New Testament in the Language of the People	1937; Reprinted 2000 as Millennium edition.

www.ingramcontent.com/pod-product-compliance
Lightning Source LLC
Chambersburg PA
CBHW071500080526
44587CB00014B/2168